JESUS CHRIST IS ALIVE AND WELL AND LIVING IN HIS CHURCH

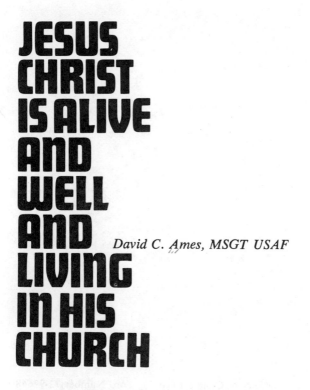

JESUS CHRIST IS ALIVE AND WELL AND LIVING IN HIS CHURCH

David C. Ames, MSGT USAF

TYNDALE HOUSE PUBLISHERS
Wheaton, Illinois

COVERDALE HOUSE PUBLISHERS LTD.
London, England

Library of Congress Catalog Card Number 72-97648
ISBN 8423-1861-5

Copyright © 1973 by Tyndale House Publishers,
Wheaton, Illinois 60187

First printing, April 1973

Printed in the United States of America

Contents

In memory of
G. Calvin Bookhardt
Assistant Fire Chief
Orlando, Florida

John 12:24—"Except a corn of wheat fall into the ground and die, it abideth alone; but if it die, it bringeth forth much fruit." In this sense, Cal Bookhardt "died" sometime in the spring of 1971, and from then on he could say with Paul, "For me to live is Christ."

His many friends and acquaintances were shocked when on December 2, 1972, he was killed in the heroic performance of his duty. His death focused the attention of the entire city on the life he had lived and on his Jesus. The spiritual repercussions have not ceased.

Preview

A lot of people have initials after their names, and it's usually to tell you something about themselves. In my case, the MSGT stands for Master Sergeant and the USAF for the United States Air Force, my employer. These initials simply show that I have little in the way of professional credentials for writing such a book as this. The civilian counterpart to my duties would be a member of a hospital administrative staff or a small office manager.

I have no affiliation with a church other than member and Sunday school teacher. I'm a layman. I can boast precious little formal education and my formal ecclesiastical education consists of a couple of night courses in a Bible college. But they were geared toward laymen, so that shouldn't ruin my amateur status.

After much searching and prayer (not all

mine), certain ideas from the Scriptures have had a tremendous impact on my life. I wrote this book so I could share with you what God is doing in me. I am one of those fellows who is perfectly happy to share anything he knows.

The quality which makes a great teacher is not brilliance, quite the contrary. Brilliant people learn too easily. They often stumble onto things without even knowing how it happened and all they know is, they know. On the other hand, I am so monumentally thickheaded as to learn only in the hardest possible way. This means, of course, that I can recount step by painful step just exactly the way to my discoveries. It is with these humble credentials that I invite you to accompany me through the discussions in this book.

If it seems that I'm being painfully honest about my qualifications or lack of them, it is for this reason: you don't have to be a theologian or a preacher to understand the abundant life. It isn't necessary to be a Ph.D. or a Four Star General to understand the "mystery" of Christ living in you. If I can grasp the subject well enough to write a book about it, then it isn't far from anyone. Just reach.

My desire for you is that you make your life available to Christ. This is the effect the Word has had on me. My life is not dedicated to my church, denomination, or a Christian organization, but to Christ. I am ready to share his message with anyone, as long as he/she is searching.

—David C. Ames

Chapter One

Searching

Jesus Christ of Nazareth is alive! Yes, he ascended into heaven and sits at the right hand of God the Father. But even more, Christ walks this earth right now.

Christ is alive and continuing his earthly ministry through Christians who make their lives available to him. The individuals he uses are not the most self-righteous, pious, or ecclesiastically educated. They are simply people who dare to believe that if God is who he says he is, then he can do what he says he can do.

The same God who can make an onion-looking affair grow into a beautiful tulip can make lives blossom. As the tulip bulb is designed to become a tulip, the spiritual seed planted in every Christian is programmed to grow into a beautiful life. A tulip bulb requires precious little help from mankind in order to mature. Someone must, of course, take it out of the package, then plant and water it. But God makes it grow.

Charting its growth or playing special tulip-growing music may be entertaining, but it won't really promote growth. All you need to do with a tulip bulb is to place it where it was intended to be placed, and it will become what it was intended to be — with God's help.

If someone mistakenly placed the tulip bulb in a bowl of water, after a week or so he might become suspicious at its lack of success and go back for a second look at the planting instructions. Christians sometimes need to take a second look at their instructions. Christ said, "I am come that they might have life, and that they might have it more abundantly" (John 10:10). And, "He that hath the Son hath life" (1 John 5:12). Yet millions of Christians are just existing, not really living. The product is not growing as expected. Faulty bulb? Or have we possibly misread the instructions?

Unfortunately some of us rarely look at the instructions for ourselves. We rely almost totally upon being taught. We are perfectly content to stake our happiness on someone else's idea of what the instructions say. Even worse, we stake the happiness of others on somebody else's interpretations, and simply pass those interpretations on without bothering to check their validity. There is no end to the possibilities of Bible misunderstandings. We could have a whole garden plot of half-grown bulbs.

My saying, "Jesus Christ is alive and well and living in his church" may imply that I think at least one denomination has read the instructions. But his church is not a denomination or an organization. It includes everyone who believes that Jesus is the Christ, the Son of the living God, the only valid atonement for sin. The church is everyone who has personally and prayerfully said, "Thank you, Lord Jesus. I am one of those sinners you died to redeem."

Most believers are affiliated with a denomination, but it would be folly to assume that all folks linked with a denomination (or a Christian organization) are true believers. This creates a problem. Suppose that Sunday school teacher whom you rely so heavily upon to spoon-feed you the Bible's instructions isn't really a Christian in the first place. He then would be a "natural man" and so not really be able to understand Bible truths (1 Corinthians 2:14), let alone communicate them.

Many religious leaders proclaim the Word of God without ever having personally met its author. I recently heard the testimony of a man who had pastored extremely large churches for fifty-two years prior to accepting Christ as his personal Savior. Now he warns Christians against the kind of do-it-yourself message that he put out during his first fifty-two years in the pulpit. He is far from alone. Thousands of preachers and priests have been saved after years in the ministry. The same holds true for deacons, elders,

Sunday school teachers, and trustees. Some never do see the light.

Even if you are sure that your preacher and Sunday school teacher are both real, "born again" believers, that still doesn't relieve you from the responsibility of searching the Scriptures for yourself.

In the military, we quote Count Helmuth von Moltke, a nineteenth-century Prussian strategist who said, "An order that can be misunderstood will be misunderstood." Von Moltke certainly didn't invent that. Satan used it six thousand years before and is still using it. He probably tells his demons, "Remember, fellows, any Scripture that can be misinterpreted will be misinterpreted by anyone not operating in the power of the Holy Spirit."

Paul's admonition in 2 Timothy 2:15 wasn't put in the Bible as a spacer: "Study to show thyself approved unto God, a workman that needeth not to be ashamed, rightly dividing the word of truth." God never intended that we get our spiritual feeding at the end of a conveyor belt.

Don't get me wrong — teaching and preaching are necessary and ordained by God, and not all teachers and preachers are suspect. But we should be motivated above the spectator level. We should be searching. Do we enter a Bible study to learn or to be entertained? Do we listen to a sermon because we hope to hear the voice of God or because it's part of the Sunday routine?

Teaching is readily available through the local

church or Christian organizations. Spiritual instruction is an integral part of the church's life and mission. But there's a problem here. The fact that Christ is really alive in his people simply isn't taught. Why and how he lived the life he lived is only imparted in half-truths. The fact that the same power responsible for Christ's victorious life is available to us isn't stressed, perhaps because the teacher isn't aware himself that such power has been at work on earth for the last 1900 years.

Rather than search for answers ourselves, we have relied on church leaders to spoon-feed us Bible knowledge, facts that those leaders sometimes can't feed us. The church is made up of too many spoon-fed Christians who don't digest the Word for themselves. We all come to church expecting an injection of spiritual truth from a teaching-preaching specialist, with no effort on our part. But if church leaders aren't able to feed us (or even if they are), we must learn to feed ourselves from the Word of God.

When the truth is not prevalent in us, what fills the void? If we forget that Christ intended to function through us, then we must conjure up an alternative belief. We can become so collectively ignorant as to forget entirely what our mission is. Some of us even act as though our task is to defend our own particular corner of Christianity. This is one result of not getting into the Bible for ourselves.

Churches and spiritual life don't always go

together. Some find the church a convenient place to hide from God. They figure that a huge stack of church paper work will keep God from noticing their lack of spiritual growth. Some think they can get so involved with church programs that the Lord won't notice the dust on their Bibles. "Somebody has to do the work," they argue. Right! (Just imagine what cataclysmic repercussions would take place if no one counted how many Bibles were brought to your church last Sunday.) But God never intended us to be spiritual paupers simply because we are too busy doing "his work."

We would like to blame our apathy on someone higher up in our "system." We would like to say that we have been infiltrated by a bunch of liberals, modernists, radicals, hippies, or whatever. The fact is that most moves to get Christians to think for themselves, read the Word, or just plain search, come from the top. But these suggestions run into a stone wall at the grass roots level. Christians sometimes don't even want to be just Christians — they want to be Methodists, Catholics, Baptists, etc.

Don't get me wrong, I'm not against denominations. It's just that they are a security blanket to too many Christians. They have become a convenient way to keep God at arm's length while we fulfil our obligations.

A recent issue of *Time* magazine printed an old quotation about Ireland, stating that it was a country with "too much religion and not enough

Christianity." That too often describes us. Unlike Ireland, we are not at war because of too much religion and not enough revolutionary Christianity. Just the opposite — we are asleep.

Today's Christian scene is not all apathy though. A spiritual awakening is affecting grassroots Christians and ecclesiastical bigwigs alike. This awakening is not a new effort by any of the "systems" or the people in them. It is due to an outpouring of the Holy Spirit such as has not been seen since the first century — perhaps because this is the last century.

Because of this spiritual awakening, there are tapes being played that are pure Bible study. Kids are wearing "Jesus the Liberator" sweat shirts. Folks who used to play bridge one night a week now don't have time because they are going to Bible studies three nights a week, plus attending church every time the doors open. White folks are sharing Christ with Blacks. White believers are inviting Blacks to church — not telling them to go to the black church, but inviting them to come to their church. I'm not talking about "carpetbag" integration engineered by Washington, but real Southern "rednecks" who have the love of Christ bubbling over in their hearts. Faith in Jesus is becoming more important than skin color.

In some places Baptists, Methodists, Catholics, and others are becoming aware that some members of other churches are actually going to the same heaven as they. They are also interested in pooling their time and resources to present Christ to kids on drugs, rather than fighting over which church they will attend when they are converted. These Christians would rather honor the Lord's command to tell everyone about Jesus and let the Holy Spirit direct the kids into a church. Unfortunately, not all Christians are catching on to this spirit of revival.

Searching is an asset. "They which do hunger and thirst after righteousness . . . shall be filled" (Matthew 5:6). Some of us come to God and gain fire insurance. Others are saved and really know how to live. That's what this book is all about — life. "I am come that they might have life, and that they might have it more abundantly" (John 10:10).

No amount of effort on our part can add this dimension to our Christian experience. We were saved from sin by God's grace, and no amount of spiritual sweat can bring us to experiential knowledge of the day-by-day victorious abundant life Jesus promised us. We were saved from something, and we were saved to something. God doesn't drop us halfway through the journey.

Too many of us think (and God hears our thoughts), "Thanks, God, for saving me. This is great. I think I'll just walk the rest of the way while I get over the shock. Besides, you've done so much already, God. I really don't feel right just riding along on your grace. Perhaps I'll get back on when I can work my passage." The trouble is, real life doesn't ultimately depend on us. No amount of human effort, no amount of sweat can do it, with one small possible exception — searching.

Maybe that sounds contradictory to you, because you think searching is work. Regardless, searching is a prerequisite. I can't think of anyone I know who has entered into this abundant life without doing some serious searching, and I think most of them would contend that it was work.

Am I trying to sell abundant life by works? Not at all. But I am saying that it's necessary to thirst and search for the abundant life. No amount of work will get you across the Jordan into the land flowing with milk and honey.

I think I can offer some keys to this paradox. For openers, searching is work only because we go up so many blind alleys. We are especially gullible for cut-and-dried methods to attain the fullness of life that eludes us. Most of these methods boil down to: "Stop enjoying life and you will be in the kingdom of heaven." If you think that self-denial in itself is the key to anything good, read Colossians 2:16-23 and "let no man beguile you of your reward in a voluntary humility."

In short we would narrow down our search and cut out a good deal of the sweat if we would simply rule out any avenue that's based on works. This would, of course, include trying to be "good," because man is incurably a rebel. He does what comes naturally — sin. If he is "good," it is unnatural and if it is unnatural, it's work and no amount of work will gain a more abundant life. Works won't do it, but searching — hungering for abundant life — will. We can't do it on our own.

What's the big deal about searching? For one thing, Satan is much more powerful than we are. He has so obscured biblical truths that we have to really want to know them to find them. Secondly, God honors searching.

Take a look at Captain Cornelius of Acts 10 fame. He was the first Gentile to become a Christian. How did he come by this honor? Was it God's good time to let the Gentiles in on a good thing and Cornelius was the ranking man in the area? Not on your life. He was searching. And his searching spirit was infectious. It caught on to all who were close to him.

I can imagine what might have transpired when a new replacement transferred into the Italian unit. "What kind of a chap is the 'old man'?" "Old Corney? He's all right, a real gentleman. But watch your language and smutty jokes. You won't make any points that way. He's a God-fearing man." Well, his sincerity even influenced God! God's angel said, "Thy prayers and thine alms have come up for a memorial before God" (Acts 10:4). Cornelius wanted to find God, and God brought him into a new life. Did Cornelius' search save him? No, but God sent Peter to tell him about Jesus. How about that for a rewarding search?

If you don't think that was dramatic enough, how about Saul of Tarsus? Saul, you may say, wasn't searching — he was killing Christians. He was sincerely doing the wrong thing, and there is a difference between self-righteously doing wrong and searchingly doing the wrong thing. Saul was protecting what he understood to be Christ by persecuting those crazy heretics who claimed that a poor ragamuffin carpenter from Nazareth was the Christ, the Messiah. Did Christ save him because of his zeal? No. But he presented himself in all his blinding glory so that Saul didn't need to search any further.

"And ye shall seek me, and find me, when ye shall search for me with all your heart" (Jeremiah 29:13). Cornelius and Paul both tried that promise and found it true.

Satan is going about "as a roaring lion . . . seeking (or searching for) whom he may devour" (1 Peter 5:8). And whom do you think he's most likely to leave alone? The enemy won't bother the self-satisfied fellow who enjoys playing church, because he thinks he's winning. Everyone respects him, his chances are good in the next deacons' election, he's happy with himself. Satan need not waste any effort with that fellow because he is no threat to the Devil's program and absolutely of no use to God's. As long as he is self-satisfied, he is in no danger of turning his life over completely to Christ.

The fellow who is lion bait is the one who is discontented, not only with his own life, but with

19

the fellows above him and the church games that they have created, or at least the ones they are profiting by. The problem is, he's not winning. Possibly no one has recognized his talents. He can make easy lion's prey if he isn't careful.

Sadder still is the Christian who started off searching and by the grace of God received some light, like the church at Philadelphia (Revelation 3:8) — "For thou hast a little strength." But he became impatient with the rest of his fellow church members who, he thought, were weaklings. Just when God was getting him to the point where he could pump some life back into that old church through him! Of course, the problem is that strangely enough no one in the church was able to recognize his new level of holiness. But he could, or at least he thought he could, and he became satisfied with himself and stopped searching. Dissatisfied with the old crowd down at the church, he dashed off to find a more enlightened crowd, one that will recognize talent when they see it.

Another reason to respect Satan's power to disguise the truth is this: it sometimes is difficult for people to grasp the message of the gospel. Simply stated, that message says: Christ died to pay a price for you that you couldn't pay for yourself, and for the asking he promised to take up residence in you, that you might have eternal life. He promised to substitute his righteousness for your unrighteousness. He promised that because he had died for your sin, you would not have to.

He promised a new life, available through him. All yours simply by accepting his offer to let him be your righteousness. No amount of work — no amount of sweat — Jesus Christ plus nothing.

Maybe you were a teen-ager, maybe older when you accepted this truth. Through these years, I'll bet you have known a lot of folks who are "working their way to heaven." You may have been one of them. Satan can cloud up a simple message like the gospel and cause folks to work and sweat for something they can actually have free.

God has given us a free gift. The very working for it would negate the offer. A gift can't be earned, it must be free. Satan may have lost the battle to keep you from being saved. But now he is fighting even harder to keep you from enjoying the full, abundant life Jesus has made available.

Chapter Two

In the Beginning—Choice

In the beginning God created choice. Before God made anything — earth, sky, or man — he had already made up his mind that man was to have a choice. Not limited choice like what color socks to wear today. God gave man complete power of selection, so complete that man could choose — or reject — God. God placed himself in a rather risky position when he armed man with such a tool. He gave man a weapon to use against God.

Can you imagine something you've made saying, "I don't want you, not even for a friend." God gave man that very option, even though he knew what man's choice would be. God knew that his creation would turn away from him, hate him. But he also realized there is no better way to prove love than by risking the alternative of rejection. Genuine love requires decision, because genuine love cannot be demanded, or- dered, or even regulated. It must be voluntary.

This tells us something about God. God doesn't do things just for kicks. He must have felt, in some sense, a need of being loved. Do you think it is fair to conclude that God "needs" us? I think so. But he never downgrades the caliber of his love by trying to force us to love him.

Not only did God authorize man to exercise the power of choice, but he also recognized what that choice — rebellion — would be and made a way back. Revelation 13:8 calls Christ "the Lamb slain from (before) the foundation of the world." Before God even started the construction of the universe, before he laid the foundation of the world, he was already making plans to send his Son into the world to die for our sins. Christ's death on the Cross was no accident. It was a way back for you and me, a way which requires a choice on our part.

Christ died for all, but not everyone has de- cided to be Christ's. Perhaps you haven't made that choice, or haven't even thought about the fact that you have one to make. Doesn't it give you a sense of importance to know that God went to all that trouble for you? He must have wanted you pretty badly. You wouldn't even be too far out to think that he needs you. Still, he left the choice with you. You have the right to walk the road to hell — despite God's wishes and desires.

Some make the objection: "God is a loving

God and wouldn't send anyone to hell." But he is a just God and won't redeem anyone against his will. "As many as received him, to them gave he power (the right) to become the sons of God" (John 1:12). God has done everything possible — except to make the decision for you. You have a decision to make and he will encourage you to believe. But he won't usurp your right of choice, no matter how badly he wants you. It's up to you.

Let's look at the first wrong choice in the history of mankind. We tend to think of it as a "slip" or a mistake, but it was more serious than that. It was very clear-cut. God didn't say anything quite so nebulous as "Be good," or, "If you go against my wishes I will be displeased." This would have made Adam wonder just what he should or shouldn't do, just what might offend God, and just what the consequences would be. God said in effect, "There is only one thing that you can do wrong. There is only one possible way you can choose against me." In Genesis 2:17 God told Adam and Eve, "But of the tree of the knowledge of good and evil, thou shalt not eat of it: for in the day that thou eatest thereof thou shalt surely die." This was his only prohibition.

Up to this point man was totally dependent upon God — not a robot, just dependent. This is what God considers the ultimate in our love affair with him, because it gives him the greatest opportunity to demonstrate his love toward us.

God knew where the breakdown would occur.

He knew that the part of man that we call "self," or his nature, would be the weak link. "Self" would simply have to have a crack at independence. Things haven't changed much; man's independent nature still gets him in trouble. Now you may not consider a little self-consideration to be a problem. But if it takes your eyes off of God, then Satan has a free hand.

The serpent said, "Look what you can do for your 'self.' You can make your 'self' as smart as God. Then you won't have to depend on God."

"Well, Mr. Serpent, God said we shouldn't eat from that tree."

"Hath God said — did he really say anything so silly? He's really out of date. Be the first one in the garden to be independent. Adam will be green with envy."

God is just. He said, "For in the day that thou eatest thereof thou shalt surely die," and they did. Not physically (at least, not immediately) — they raised a family and dead folks can't do that. Their souls hadn't died. Mind, emotion, and will make up the soul. The soul is where the real you lives. There is little doubt in anyone's mind that this facet of man was passed on to all of Adam's descendants.

Man's death was, of course, spiritual, but even that needs some ironing out. Death was spiritual and yet unregenerate persons — strangers to Christ — possess spirits of their own. This may not hit you just right, because you have always thought of man as body and soul only. Any reference to spirit was automatically interpreted to be the Holy Spirit. No so. See 1 Corinthians 2:11.

You cannot always identify "spirit" in the Bible as the Holy Spirit. The Bible contrasts the spirit of man with the Holy Spirit. The 1 Corinthians passage is not by any means the only Scripture demonstrating the spirit of man. If you are in doubt and have a concordance, I suggest you check the references on the word "spirit." You may be surprised at the number of times it obviously refers to man's spirit rather than the Holy Spirit. I was rather a diehard on this subject. There is nothing wrong with the "Show me" approach to any doctrine. Paul commended the Bereans because they "searched the Scriptures daily, whether those things were so" (Acts 17: 11).

The term "spirit of man" may, at first look, seem totally inaccurate, especially if you were getting along quite well not even aware of its existence. Not to have a spirit would be rather like trying to plug in your toaster without having a plug or wire. The Holy Spirit serves a similar function because it is through the Spirit that man and God commune. He is the connection. If you want man to come spiritually alive, first you justify him, pay the price for his sin, clean him up. Then you connect God's Spirit into man's spirit and watch the power of God flow in. That's the reverse of what happened to Adam. He cut himself off from the Holy Spirit, pulled his own cord.

Man has no storage battery which will allow him to function independently, but he sure tries. Adam exercised his prerogative just exactly the way God knew he would, and mankind went down the tubes as far as a relationship with God is concerned.

The first Adam brought death. Through the second Adam, Christ, we receive life. God sent his Son to take our punishment, and when we choose Christ as our Savior, we are covered by his atoning work. By choice we are justified, made right with God.

If we compare ourselves with Adam after the fall, we find that, like him, we have body, soul and spirit. If we have by choice accepted God's offer of justification, we gain an additional component, the Holy Spirit. John 14:16, 17 tells us, "And I will pray the Father, and he shall give you another Comforter, that he may abide with you forever; even the Spirit of truth; whom the world cannot receive, because it seeth him not, neither knoweth him: but ye know him; for he dwelleth with you, and shall be in you." Ephesians 4:30 adds that we are sealed by the Holy Spirit "unto the day of redemption." He makes us spiritually alive.

The only way for man to be spiritually alive is to be personally related to God by faith. Adam had known his Maker in a person-to-person relationship, but the fall disrupted this fellowship.

When he repented, he came to know God by faith. Similarly, you and God were strangers until you turned to him in faith, at which time your fellowship with God began.

But the choices don't stop with accepting Christ as Savior. I know a lot of Christians (like myself) who wasted many years with wrong choices. We understand why God gave us the capability of choice, but many of us probably wish he had forced us to behave according to his plan once we were his.

We have salvation — some call it "fire insurance." We love God because he will put us in heaven some day. We would like to represent God better, but — well, in this day and age, "old-time religion" is out of style.

Isn't that great? We have Fire Insurance. God put us in a fireproof bag, sealed us, and put us on the shelf to await his Son's return. That last statement is ridiculously close to what some folks think the Christian life is all about.

People who have been adopted as sons or daughters of God will certainly not spend eternity in hell. So you could, from that standpoint, consider salvation Fire Insurance. We are sealed, but not in a fireproof bag. And if we're on the shelf of idleness, it's not because God put us there.

Before you were saved by God's grace, you were totally independent — independent of God, anyway. You might be surprised to learn who was actually controlling your life while you thought you were at the controls. You were independent because Adam by his own choice told God to leave him alone. God did, but Satan didn't.

God sent his Son into the world to redeem sinners. "Redeem" doesn't mean to save from hell. It means to restore to the original position and purpose, which also includes going to heaven some day. If you are in a fireproof bag on the shelf, waiting for heaven, you are enjoying only part of what God has provided for you.

Partly saved? No, being saved is like being pregnant. You either are or aren't, and no one was ever slightly saved or slightly pregnant. If, however, the number of pregnancies that develop into mature human beings, able to reproduce, corresponded to the maturing of spiritual rebirths, the next United Nations General Assembly meeting could be held in a one-room apartment.

Many Christians just don't seem to mature enough to reproduce.

You may have heard it said that the fruit of a Christian is another Christian. I feel that this is an unfortunate cliché, because it implies that if you're not a soul winner, then you haven't grown spiritually. Not so. It doesn't work in reverse either. No one should feel he has "arrived" because he has been able to bring someone to God.

Nevertheless, the idea that spiritual maturity and spiritual reproduction go hand in hand is not without some validity, just as the ability to physically reproduce implies a certain level of physical maturity. Neither certifies maximum maturity by a long shot.

My point is probably becoming clear by now. Think of all the Christians you know. Now think of all the believers that you are sure have been used to lead someone to Christ. No, I don't want you to categorize your friends. This is not an assessment or judgment. Don't try to think of all the ones who you believe have not led someone to Christ, or why they haven't. Just roughly, what do you think the percentage of soul-winning Christians is? Pretty low? I think you're right.

I'm sure all believers were intended to be soul winners. I can see precious little reason for God's leaving us here other than that he wants to use our lives to tell others about what he has to offer. Yes, I also know he wants us to specialize. Soul-winning may not be your "bag," but you play the organ or are the custodian. God uses organists and janitors to lead folks to Christ, as well as preachers and Sunday school teachers. He uses them, that is, if they are available.

Back to the basic premise: Christians often don't produce other Christians, simply because they don't mature spiritually. Central to this matter of Christian maturity is choice. We still exercise an option. If we choose not to mature, we won't.

As Christians we belong to God. But we can still act independently, and when we do, we choose to steal or hoard. Or maybe you would rather say, "misappropriate." Weeds by any other name are still weeds. In 1 Corinthians 6: 19, 20 we are informed that our bodies house the Holy Spirit and that he did not barge in like an unwanted relative. God purchased the residence (me) just for the purpose of displaying his love.

We are all familiar with the mother-in-law image that comedians have been using for years. She moves in for a "visit," and takes charge, rearranges the furniture, changes the menu, and decides how to raise the kids. Well, God isn't like that (and neither are most mothers-in-law). Sometimes we wish he were. After all, he owns us now, so why doesn't he take over? We can go right back to Adam's situation for the answer. God gave Adam a choice of independence, because true love can't be forced, demanded, or regulated. It must by its very nature be spontaneous.

Perhaps it was a desire to avoid being owned by Satan that caused us to give ourselves to God. But anyway we accepted Christ's atoning death as the price for our sins. Even though God now owns us, he still won't grab the controls away from "self." We must choose to relinquish control day by day and moment by moment.

There are times when we would like to say once and for all, "You take over the controls, God, because I am tried of making a bad job of it." We would like Christian living to be like salvation, when we by faith alone accepted God's offer to become sons of God. Once and for all, and that was it. Daily decisions to live for Christ are by faith too, but they need continual renewing. That in itself has a certain beauty about it.

When my wife told me that she would accept my offer to share my life with her, nothing would ease my mind until we were married. I wanted to make it final before someone with more to offer came along and changed her mind. My concern was purely selfish and had its origin in insecurity. God is not insecure. He knows that what he has to offer can't be beat. He doesn't hit you on the head with his plan to keep you on his side. God has enough confidence in his blueprint for your life that he doesn't try to force it on you.

In the beginning God created man to willingly love him, and you demonstrate true love every time you choose to be dependent on God's pure love. That's beautiful!

words that we as men might choose. So we use the Holy Spirit's words to explain the Holy Spirit's facts. (14) But the man who isn't a Christian can't understand and can't accept these thoughts from God, which the Holy Spirit teaches us. They sound foolish to him, because only those who have the Holy Spirit within them can understand what the Holy Spirit means. Others just can't take it in. (15) But the spiritual man has insight into everything, and that bothers and baffles the man of the world, who can't understand him at all. (16) How could he? For certainly he has never been one to know the Lord's thoughts, or to discuss them with him, or to move the hands of God by prayer. But, strange as it seems, we Christians actually do have within us a portion of the very thoughts and mind of Christ. (1) Dear brothers, I have been talking to you as though you were still just babies in the Christian life, who are not following the Lord, but your own desires; I cannot talk to you as I would to healthy Christians, who are filled with the Spirit. (2) I have had to feed you with milk and not with solid food, because you couldn't digest anything stronger. And even now you still have to be fed on milk. (3) For you are still only baby Christians, controlled by your own desires, not God's. When you are jealous of one another and divide up into quarreling groups, doesn't that prove you are still babies, wanting your own way? In fact, you are acting like people who don't belong to the Lord at all. (4) There you are, quarreling about whether I am greater than Apollos, and dividing the church. Doesn't this show how little you have grown in the Lord?   (*The Living Bible*)

You will see that these ten verses contain a wealth of knowledge about man that every Christian (and non-Christian) should know. Besides the two kinds of Christians mentioned, there is also a person who does not know God, sometimes called the natural or unspiritual man. He is unsaved, unregenerate, and exactly like Adam after the fall. Every man since Adam has been in the same condition. He is naturally alive but spiritually dead, and therefore ignorant of spiritual things (see verse 14).

Verse 11 tells us the natural man cannot understand the things of God without being specially equipped. In this day of specialization we certainly understand the requirement of special equipment for special jobs. Studying the Bible, living a Christian life, and doing God's work are special jobs and require special equipment — the Spirit of God.

It isn't hard for us to see why the natural man is so spiritually ignorant. But we Christians are different; we are equipped. We are sealed with the Holy Spirit (Ephesians 4:30). A sealed unit sounds infallible, incapable of breakdown. But . . .

We're familiar with specialized equipment in this age of specialization, but we are even better acquainted with equipment breakdown and component failure. Don't get me wrong. No one ever had a faulty Holy Spirit component installed at his spiritual rebirth. But a poor connection is a possibility.

But that is not caused by the manufacturer. God cannot be accused of sloppy craftsmanship. We can, however, be guilty of neglect. We must understand that the Holy Spirit is not just equipment given to us by God. He is himself God living in us both to will and to do his good pleasure. Our spiritual laziness can result in a poor connection with the indwelling Spirit.

Likening God the Holy Spirit to an inanimate object for the sake of teaching has been done before. The Bible uses oil as a symbol of the Holy Spirit to illustrate his activity in us. Man's spirit is spoken of in the Bible as a lamp, and God's Spirit dwelling within us is the oil or fuel. It's not really the lamp that makes the light, but the oil. If the lamp gives off a dim light, we trim the wick, not the oil.

Sometimes a believer looks and acts more like a natural man than a Christian. He has the special equipment, but simply doesn't use it. He is the "baby" Christian of 1 Corinthians 3. Some believers don't like to admit that the "baby," or carnal, Christian is part of the family, but he is. How does a Christian become carnal anyway? What causes the poor connection? Sin.

1 and 2 Corinthians were, of course, written to the church in Corinth. The church was not just a social gathering as it sometimes is today. It included believers only, because it was not fashionable to belong to a church. In fact, it was dangerous. The major problem of the Corinthians was sin, unconfessed and unrepented sin (1 Corinthians 3:1).

The Apostle John told Christians, in 1 John 1:9, "If we confess our sins, he is faithful and just to forgive us our sins, and to cleanse us from all unrighteousness." If we sin as Christians, we need forgiveness and cleansing.

We never need a second helping of justification. We don't need to be saved all over again. God is a loving God, and Christ paid for all the sins that we committed up to the time we were saved and all the sins we will commit until the day of final redemption. Our salvation was provided once for all. But because he is just, God will not fellowship with a son or daughter of his who stubbornly refuses to confess his/her sin.

Sin is the corrosion that causes a short in our spiritual system. Sin will break the spiritual connection. We still belong to God, but don't have the benefit of his fellowship.

The carnal Christian is a child of the King, but doesn't enjoy the benefits because of sins in his life. He is allowing his own disobedience to stand between himself and his heavenly Father. How can he show God love when he won't even talk to God?

To get a complete picture, let's look at the other Christian. The normal Christian life is mentioned in 1 Corinthians 2:15 — "he that is spiritual." What a contrast between the two. Paul says the carnal man is full of envying, strife, etc. But in Galatians 5:22, 23 he tells us that Christian character consists of "love, joy, peace, longsuffering, gentleness, goodness, faith, meekness, and temperance."

Since it's sin that separates us from God, puts us out of fellowship, and causes us to become carnal (fleshly), maybe we should make sure we understand what sin really is.

What is sin? Smoking, drinking, or chewing tobacco? Or wearing short skirts, lipstick, or false eyelashes? All of these have been preached against at one time or another by folks who would have us believe that Christianity is nothing but a list of don'ts. This is not Christianity — it is negativism, a poor advertisement for Christianity.

Sin is *anything* in our thoughts, words, or deeds that is contrary to the will of God. Some items may vary from Christian to Christian. Why should this be? All believers have the same God! Yes, but he gives us all different work in different areas. And we don't all grow at the same rate.

Earlier we referred to Colossians 2:16-23, which warns against ordinances of "touch not, taste not, handle not." What is the danger in a negative code? None in itself, but frequently we get proud of what we don't do. The next thing is to form a select circle around our abstinences, so we can be proud together.

This is a terrible pitfall. We have grown so accustomed to judging a fellow Christian's growth by what he doesn't do that we have created an open door for proud phonies. If you doubt this, think about it for a moment. How do we even know that so and so doesn't do a majority of these things unless he tells us?

Sometimes someone accepts Christ, and "old things are passed away; behold, all things are become new." But if he ignores the guidance of the Holy Spirit, he'll do as the natural man does. He'll just go along with what is socially acceptable in his new environment.

First he learns some Christian catch phrases like "Praise the Lord" or "Amen, brother." Then he meets someone who has a ready-made list of sins for him to start not doing. He can watch his progress and know just what caliber or rank Christian he is by the things he's given up. Neat. Satan can save his energy when Christians allow pride to blunt their testimony.

I have actually met people who wanted Christ as their Savior but put it off because they knew they couldn't give up "all that" just yet. I'm not talking about folks who weren't ready to repent, but who just weren't ready to accept someone's staggering list of dos and don'ts. They just didn't feel up to it. Surprisingly enough, it's hard to convince these people that Christianity is not just a series of taboos.

Define sin again: Anything that is contrary to the will of God. That gets tough. It all boils down to this — your will or his. God's will (more specifically, God's character) is the standard of right and wrong, not some man-made list.

We know that we have freedom in Christ, and that these no-no lists are part of man's attempts to soothe his conscience through religion. But the Holy Spirit may have a reason for telling us to go along with them. If that is what he says to us, then nothing short of that will do. God may be planning to show them through us that they don't need their lists. They wouldn't listen to us though if they thought we were only defending our own position.

The important thing to remember is that sin is whatever is contrary to God's will *for you*. One of the jobs of the Holy Spirit is to convict us of sin. Our job, then, in order to maintain a right relationship with God, is to confess the sin as soon as the Holy Spirit points to its presence in our lives. If we confess it, our relationship is immediately restored. If we don't, we are simply out of touch with God.

When we are habitually in fellowship with God, we are living a spiritual life. When we are out of fellowship, we are carnal Christians. We cannot grow when we are out of fellowship. We remain "babes in Christ."

Is there any limit to the depths of sin that a carnal Christian can commit? Perhaps when a Christian gets too far out of line, God will simply take him home. Nowhere are we told that a man who resists the Holy Spirit dwelling within him will act or react any differently than a man who doesn't have the Holy Spirit at all.

Some folks maintain that if someone does this or that, he just wasn't saved in the first place. We would like to think that we are immune to what we might consider "real bad sin," but remember, God won't force his will on even his own children. Generally speaking, the farther out in the world a Christian lives, the more apt he is to want to do some "way out" things — things that are far from the will of God for him.

I'm not trying to let you know how much you can get away with as a Christian. I'm just pointing out how much we can bungle the job when we try to live in our own strength, independently of God. The cure for this situation is, of course, 1 John 1:9, which cannot be overemphasized because no one on earth outgrows his need of forgiveness.

Well, that's simple. When we go to bed at night, we can say a blanket prayer of confession like, "Now I lay me down to sleep, forgive me of my sins. Amen." No, that won't cut it. Why wait until you go to bed at night to get right with God? We are told to "grieve not the Holy Spirit of God" (Ephesians 4:30) — and to save our unconfessed sin definitely grieves the Holy Spirit. Why? Because God created man to love him, and man can't return God's love if he is out of fellowship. And, obviously, we ought to be specific in our confession of sin.

1 John 1:9 states clearly that if we confess our sins, he will forgive us and cleanse us. Confess. That is the key word here. This means a couple of things. One is to cite or name the act (omission or commission) and then to call it what God calls it — sin.

You see, we have no assurance that we can receive forgiveness just by asking for it. In fact, quite the contrary, 1 John 1:9 doesn't even say to ask for forgiveness. It says to genuinely confess the sin to God, and forgiveness is automatic.

One word of caution. 1 John 1:9 also says nothing about repentance, but throughout the Bible we see that God examines man's motives and desires. It would seem rather foolish to expect God to forgive us of a sin that we're not really sorry for or don't really intend to discontinue. This doesn't mean you can't expect forgiveness if "it" ever happens again. I'm talking about the "Oh, well, I'll just confess it" attitude. That's dangerous.

"Do you mean God will forgive even *that?*" some might ask. Yes, even *that.* Of course, I don't have any idea what your *that* is, but I know that whatever it is, my God is big enough to forgive it. "Do you mean he will forgive *that* that many times?" Yes, that many times. Don't ever be ashamed to come to God with a besetting sin. It seems that this is God the Holy Spirit's way of breaking us of some of our most persistent sins.

It is clear that the carnal Christian was not the

ultimate result God had in mind when he sent his Son into the world to redeem man. God never intended to primarily use either the carnal or natural man in his program. The carnal Christian is a round peg in a square hole. Incredibly, Christianity has sometimes designed holes to fit the pegs that are available — carnal pegs. Churches put carnal Christians to work for two reasons: They far outnumber the spiritual Christians, and being involved might help them to grow.

Designing slots to utilize carnal Christians has caused a lot of heartache both to God and to fellow believers, but not nearly as much as having a carnal Christian fill a spot designed to be filled by a totally spiritual individual.

Having God at the controls — that is what being spiritual is all about. If God's plan was to redeem you so he could use you to spread his Good News, then "he that is spiritual" is he that is available. As opposed to the carnal Christian, the spiritual man is dead to self and alive to God's plan. He has come to grips with the question of just what he will and won't do. He (or she) will do anything that God wants, regardless of whether or not the position is beneath his/her dignity. The spiritual Christian has made his choice. He knows that he could have said no to God, but he has decided never to shut out God again.

It sounds like a high price, a demanding sacrifice. But all who have paid the price assure us it was the best investment of their lives.

Chapter Four

Jesus Power

King David lived way back in ancient history, but his example speaks to us today. David committed some mighty serious sins, but he found forgiveness. Obviously, his sin wasn't a good example, but he demonstrated what to do about it. David bounced right back into God's service by admitting his disobedience. He momentarily fell to sin, but he wasn't defeated by it. He was knocked down, but not out.

Some Christians don't know about 1 John 1:9, and are convinced that because they are such fleshly Christians, God has no use for them. Teaching Sunday school classes, singing in the choir, visiting the sick should be done by the "good" Christians. If only they knew the power of confession!

Not confessing sin and thereby grieving the Holy Spirit is what makes a Christian carnal. We sin because we are sinners, and unless we are living in the Spirit we will walk in the flesh — and the flesh compulsively sins. One of the most important things we can learn as Christians is to be ready to confess sin, to keep short accounts with God.

By contrast, Christ never once had to ask to be forgiven. He was perfect. So what can we possibly learn from Christ's thirty-three years on this earth?

Romans 3:20 tells us, "Therefore by the deeds of the law there shall no flesh be justified in his sight: for by the law is the knowledge of sin." All the law could do was to show us what failures we were. The law is a yardstick. It doesn't tell us how to be good or how to successfully live a Christian life, but how far short we fall of God's standards.

If the Son of God came to earth and lived a perfect life with regard to the law and kept every commandment every day of his life, what can we learn from that? That he was perfect. The law has already told us that we aren't perfect. But that is why Christ's life had to be sinless — so he could save my imperfect life.

This sometimes discourages me, though. Christ is the law personified, and when I look for encouragement I find a standard far from my reach. To top it off, Christ not only demonstrates that the standard can be met, but he teaches me that if I even think evil, I have sinned. Then for good measure he throws in "love one another" (John 13:34).

If all the rest wasn't impossible, that last commandment would do me in. Try as I may, there are a lot of "one anothers" running around that I don't love. No doubt about it — I fall far short of God's perfection as attained by Jesus Christ.

And yet Christ the man on earth was no more than God intends *us* to be. Run that by again! I know that may sound sacrilegious to some. Do I doubt the unique deity of Christ? No. He was God, but to perform his earthly mission he left behind his glory and power and became a man who was totally dependent upon his heavenly Father.

Let's look at some pertinent Scripture. Philippians 2:5-11 explains this paradox. Check out verse 6: "He thought it not robbery to be equal with God" — because he is God. Verse 7 says, "But [he] made himself of no reputation, and took upon him the form of a servant, and was made in the likeness of men." Verse 8 tells us, "He humbled himself, and became obedient unto death." As God he didn't need to obey, but as man he did. Hebrews 5:8 reports, "Though he were a Son, yet learned he obedience." As a true man, Jesus learned obedience by rejecting disobedience, a totally foreign test to one who is only God.

Therefore when he became obedient unto death, even the death of the Cross (Philippians 2:8), it was not because he was God. It was because he was a totally obedient, dependent, available man. That's Jesus Christ our example.

This same passage comes across clearer in *The Living Bible*: ". . . Jesus Christ, who, though he was God, did not demand and cling to his rights as God, but laid aside his mighty power and glory, taking the disguise of a slave and becoming like men. And he humbled himself even further, going so far as actually to die a criminal's death on a cross."

Because Christ lived a perfect life and gave it up for our sakes, we are justified; we can have victory over the grave. Because he accomplished this in complete obedience as the God-Man, we can have victory over the power of sin. Christ set aside the power of his own deity, choosing rather to be fortified by God the Holy Spirit — who also indwells believers — and so lived a perfect life and accomplished the will of his Father. Do you get the full implication of that? Jesus used no power not available to *us*. Don't just shake this off — think it through.

Jesus Christ could have called ten thousand angels to his aid. But if he had he would have been exercising his divine prerogative at the expense of his human dependence and so he would have defied his Father's plan. That would have been sin. Jesus became man so God the Father could act through him. When we give anything a higher priority rating than the will of God, we make our lives unavailable to God the Holy Spirit who wants to accomplish his work on earth through us.

Christ claimed to represent the Father. "The Son can do nothing of himself" (John 5:19). "I can of mine own self do nothing . . . I seek not mine own will, but the will of the Father which hath sent me" (John 5:30). "As the living Father hath sent me, and I live by the Father; so he that eateth me, even shall he live by me" (John 6:57). "Jesus answered them and said, My doctrine is not mine, but his that sent me. If any man will do his will, he shall know of the doctrine, whether it be of God, or whether I speak of myself. He that speaketh of himself seeketh his own glory: but he that seeketh his glory that sent him, the same is true, and no unrighteousness is in him" (John 7:16-18).

Let's zero in on a specific miracle in John 11 — the raising of Lazarus. Jesus' statement in verse 4 seems to contradict what we have been saying — "This sickness is not unto death, but for the glory of God, that the Son of God might be glorified thereby."

First, none of this was an accident, but a demonstration of God's power. Second, both the Father and the Son were to be glorified. But didn't Christ often say he was not representing himself but the Father? Why, then, should Christ expect the "Son of God" to be "glorified?" This glory for Christ was not an end in itself — it was for credibility.

Christ was concerned about people believing

him — so the Father would be glorified. Jesus took his time arriving on the scene, telling his disciples beforehand that Lazarus was dead. He showed his grief at the death. Then, when it had been established that not only was Lazarus dead, but his body was decomposing, Jesus publicly prayed and thanked God.

Christ indicated that he prayed to clarify the source of his power, so that all present would know who was to receive the glory and in whose power the miracle was performed.

Maybe this seems to be splitting hairs. You may say this sounds like government bureaus simply transferring assets from one department to another as equals. Jesus truly is the "only begotten Son" of God (John 3:16) — issuing from, not created by God. But Jesus "was made a little lower than the angels" (Hebrews 2:9) so he as a true man could live the holy life by the same power available to us — the Holy Spirit.

It took me sixteen years to recognize that Jesus died for me and six more years to find how he lived for me. That makes me a retarded Christian. But now I'm living by the power that worked in Jesus' life — the power of the Spirit of God.

Chapter Five

The Only Good Christian Is a Dead Christian

As Christians we are perfect in Christ. But we do not always choose to be for Christ.

We are justified in Christ. This is why we could call salvation "fire insurance." Have you ever believed that you were a miserable sinner, hopelessly lost, and that Christ died to save you from this condition? Did you choose to accept him into your heart and life? If you did, then you have been justified, made righteous in God's sight.

The wording of that last paragraph on justification was all in the past tense. This is because justification is based not only on what Christ did two thousand years ago, but on what you did by way of choice, and it separates you for spiritual blessings you will receive.

Unfortunately, the "blessings" and the "you will" are all too often projected as "heaven some day." We evangelicals have majored on justification as if it were a ticket to heaven but nothing more. Of course, if we are saved we are justified back into God's presence, which authorizes us entrance to heaven some day. But that is only one side of the gospel message: unfortunately we have given it out as if it were the whole thing in a nutshell. "Step right up, folks. Get your free ticket to heaven." The new life God offers us involves more than a pass to paradise.

Why did God create man? To love his Maker and to fellowship with him. He gave man a moral choice. God knew what man's choice would be, but loved him so much he prepared a way back. He didn't justify man back into his presence just for a heaven some day. God justifies men and women for love and fellowship now. A Christian who sees heaven some day as the prime target in justification sees his ultimate destiny but misses the point of life today.

We have just about worn out the word "justification." Let's go to work on another word which is much avoided because it is little understood and therefore controversial — "sanctification."

According to Webster, to sanctify is to make holy, to set apart, or "to give sanction to the intention." What was God the Father's intention in justifying us through Christ the Son? It was that he might through the indwelling Holy Spirit use our lives, which he purchased, to do his work and will on earth. If we are totally available to him, then we are serving the purpose for which he redeemed us. If "self" is at the helm, we are not functioning as God intended redeemed man to function. Thus, if we are available to God for whatever he wishes of us, we are experiencing sanctification.

What about the holy part? God is holy and if we are set apart so he can live through us, we will be holy. You might say being wholly available goes with being holy.

While justification rests on what you have done with Jesus (past tense), sanctification depends on what you are doing with Jesus (present tense). So you asked him to save you sometime in the past. Fine! But are you letting him take control of your life now?

Christ completely in control of your life; you being a hundred percent available twenty-four hours a day for the slightest wish and command of the one who redeemed you — that's sanctification.

"It's all well and good to talk about letting Christ take over, but I know I'll keep on doing things that I shouldn't." That's because the "old man" grabs the controls for a while. Don't think you're alone. Even the Apostle Paul said, in Romans 7:19, "For the good that I would, I do not: but the evil which I would not, that I do." If God's choice servant Paul could admit that he had a problem controlling his old nature, then I should not be ashamed to admit that I fall short too.

Paul also said, in the prior verse, that "in me

(that is, in my flesh) dwelleth no good thing."
What is flesh anyway? We know that the spirit
is willing, but the flesh is weak (Matthew 26:
41). But we sometimes make the mistake of
equating flesh with the body. It's not our bodies
that stand in the way of our spiritual growth, it's
our wills.

God accomplishes his ministry on earth through
your body and mine. He uses your lips to tell
your neighbor about salvation, your feet to carry
you to him, your hands to do him a good deed
prior to witnessing so that the witness carries
some weight. Flesh is "self," the "old man" or
Adamic nature. It is internal, not external. Flesh
is not what you see in the mirror, but it may be
the reason you look.

The Bible has a lot to say about what God
thinks of our "selves," but one Scripture well rep-
resents the whole group. Isaiah 64:6 says, "But
we are all as an unclean thing, and all our righteousnesses are as filthy rags; and we all do fade
as a leaf; and our iniquities, like the wind, have
taken us away." God sees our righteousnesses as
filthy rags. The best we have is fit only for the
trash can. If in our flesh we have no good thing,
why should we let flesh have a go at running our
lives? "Therefore, brethren, we are debtors not
to the flesh, to live after the flesh" (Romans 8:
12).

The only good Christian is a dead Christian.
Not a dead body, not a dead mind, but a dead
"self." The abundant life is not working over

"self" until it can mimic Christ — it is crucifying "self" so that Christ can show through.

But how can we kill the "old man"? We know he has an Adamic nature, and has been condemned by God. But we can't do him in, try as we may. No amount of effort, no amount of sweat can get rid of the "old man."

Read Romans 6:6 — "Knowing this, that our old man is crucified with him, that the body of sin might be destroyed, that henceforth we should not serve sin." When Christ was crucified, our "old man" died along with him. You say that "old man" is the liveliest dead thing you ever saw? There is a reason for this.

Salvation and sanctification have an important point in common. Christ's death on the Cross was not effective for you until you believed and accepted it. What about the crucifixion of the "old man"? We are told in Romans 6:11, "So look upon your old sin nature as dead and unresponsive to sin, and instead be alive to God, alert to him through Jesus Christ our Lord." We are to consider ourselves dead to sin in order to get the "old man" away from the controls and allow Christ through the Holy Spirit to have full control.

Jesus Christ's own example helps us. The Holy Spirit descended on Christ at the time of his baptism. This happened in visible manner ("like a dove"), so that all generations would know that he did indeed possess the Holy Spirit. He was to use the Spirit's power in his ministry, thus setting a tremendous example for us.

There was more than one reason for Christ's baptism, but one was so he could demonstrate his death to "self" — his putting the will of God before personal needs and desires.

Hebrews 4:15 reminds us, "For we have not an high priest which cannot be touched with the feeling of our infirmities; but was in all points tempted like as we are, yet without sin."

After Jesus' baptism he took a forty-day trip into the wilderness to be tempted by Satan. Sometimes I wonder whether Jesus was tempted to do some of the same things that Satan catches me on? Was Jesus ever tempted to do some of the things that cause me to fall? If I have a problem with telling white lies on my income tax return or exceeding the speed limit, was Jesus tempted to do similar things? The Bible says he was "in all points tempted like as we are."

A temptation always plays on a person's usual desires. For instance, if I offer my wife a plate of fresh oysters, she would not only be untempted, she would unflinchingly dump them in the garbage. She simply doesn't like oysters. On the other hand, if I offer her an ice cream cone when she is on one of her diets, that would be a horse of a different flavor. She might not indulge, but she would definitely be tempted.

As the divine Son of God, Christ had the power to turn stones into bread. I'm not so sure, however, that the real issue was Christ's being hungry after his forty-day fast. I feel that the real temptation was much closer to home for Jesus. You see, Jesus chose not to use his own deity, choosing rather to operate in his Father's deity through the Holy Spirit.

In this case, Christ had to choose between performing a miracle in his own right and so get Satan off his back, or else wait upon the Spirit. Now it looks a lot more tempting. It wasn't easy for someone with all the power of the universe at his finger tips to quote Scripture and wait upon the Spirit, while Satan was trying his best to provoke him. Satan never stopped trying, even at Calvary, making men taunt, "Come on down from the cross if you are the Son of God!" (Matthew 27:40). Of course, Jesus could have, but he didn't.

This is, I believe, the real crux of Christ's being in all points tempted like as we are. We are tempted to run our own lives, and if we fall for that one we are a pushover for whatever Satan throws at us. If it seems that Christ could of his own self do nothing, it was because he had chosen to make himself completely and totally available to God the Father for his use. Anything less would have been to go against the will of the Father and therefore would have been sin. This, of course, is what Satan wanted.

If Satan can make you a "self"-controlled Christian, then you are not a Spirit-controlled Christian. Spirit-controlled Christians are the only kind that pose any problem to Satan, because he knows well that they are the only ones that God can effectively use to accomplish his work.

Christ died to "self," but for different reasons than we should. We find that our "self" cannot do the job, God has condemned it, and "self" stands in the way of God working through us. Christ's death to "self" wasn't for these reasons. He is sinless. The Son of Man acted exactly as God always intended man to act — totally dependent on God.

Christ stated that his doctrine was not his own, but the Father's who sent him (John 7:16). He could say this without reservation because he wasn't concerned only about himself. He didn't have to stop and think it over before he spoke. He went on to say in verse 18 that anyone who spoke of himself was seeking his own glory, but if one sought the glory of him who sent him, no unrighteousness was in him.

That could be you, if you have put "self" on the Cross. 2 Corinthians 5:15 tells us, "He died for all, that they which live should not henceforth live unto themselves. . . ." The only good Christian is a dead Christian.

Chapter Six

What Can I Do for an Encore?

I gave my life to Christ — so what's next?
Now I can enjoy life at its best, but what can I do
about that "self" that keeps pulling me down?

As I reach out for a fuller Christian life I sometimes find little tidbits here and there that seem to
contribute or seem to be the answer, but nothing
spectacular happens. I find a Scripture here and
a Scripture there that seems to point ever closer.
I go back and forth, up and down in my search.
I am whipped into a frenzy of excitement by
some new fact I've stumbled upon. I experience
anxious moments as a brother or sister searcher
shares his/her latest "find," only to experience
that sinking fear that maybe God has had it with
me. Maybe as a Christian I've fought the Spirit
too much for God to ever really use me again.
God has been patient with me long enough.

This is, of course, foolish thinking. How long

was God patient with us in presenting his salvation message to us? God doesn't give up on us overnight, though it is also true that he deals firmly with our stubbornness.

If you are still searching, that's proof enough that there is yet hope. There are plenty of Christians in danger of never entering into the abundant life — because of apathy. If they think they have a full understanding and know all they need to know, then complacency takes over. Complacency is Satan's best tool to keep Christians from ever becoming what God intended them to be. The fact that you are reading this book may indicate you are searching for something better. Perhaps you feel that God intended the Christian life to be something more than you are experiencing. If this is so, then you are definitely still in the running.

Do you know who it was the people chose as head man in the golden calf episode of Exodus 32? Moses' brother Aaron. In fact, he didn't even try to talk the people out of it. Imagine making a god in the shape of a cow and then saying that this is what brought them out of Egypt. If God ever got furious with anyone, he surely had a right to be so with Aaron. God slew about three thousand people because of this sin, but he didn't slay Aaron. Do you know why? Because when Moses said in verse 26, "Who is on the Lord's side?" Aaron repented and returned to the Lord's side, and God used Aaron even after that! You can be on the Lord's side — and if you're not, you're against him.

If you're convinced that God hasn't written you off as hopeless, we'll go on. What are we looking for anyway? We know that some Christians have lives that are used of Christ and some don't. We know that there is something different about the Apostle Paul, D. L. Moody, Billy Graham, and some believers we know. There is something more and we want it. How do we know when we have it?

This is a touchy question. Right here we can easily fall flat on our faces, or get sidetracked. There are those who would tell you quickly that being sanctified or entering into the abundant life is the same as being filled with the Holy Ghost. This is true.

Some would go one step further and claim that because this is so, you must speak in tongues when you receive the filling. They would back up their statement by citing several verses in Acts. I do not mean to discredit those who claim the gift of tongues, nor to imply that it is not of the Lord. Some outstanding Christians speak in tongues, and it is evident to all that Christ is a vital part of their lives.

Some Christians do teach that tongues and the filling of the Holy Ghost come necessarily as a package deal. To propagate such a doctrine is to say that no one ever was or will be Spirit-filled without this sign of tongues. 1 Corinthians 12:30 demolishes this viewpoint by asking, "Do all speak in tongues?" The context shows that the obvious answer is, no.

David Wilkerson, author of *The Cross and the Switchblade,* who himself prays in tongues, says: "And when a brother in Christ comes to me and says, 'I believe I too have received a wonderful Holy Ghost baptism and I've never spoken with tongues,' I say, 'Praise God! I believe you.' Why should there be any argument? We should rejoice in each other's love for Christ.

"I believe the Holy Ghost is big enough to take care of himself. He needs no defense, no super-salesmen, no public relations director, and no pressure promoting. And I don't believe in Holy Ghost specialists who spend their time promoting the gift instead of the Giver."*

Nothing in the Word indicates that Christ ever spoke in tongues. Perhaps he didn't need to. The Holy Spirit descended on him in the form of a dove, which was accreditation enough. Excluding tongues at Pentecost (where they were used also as a means of communication), tongues were mainly given as a sign. This is the only reason we are even discussing this phenomenon, because it was a sign and that is what we are talking about — signs of abundant life.

There can be no doubt, as seen in Acts, that tongues played a very important role in the early church. The classic instance of this sign came

*From *The Cross and the Switchblade* magazine, June 1972. Used by permission of David Wilkerson Youth Crusades.

with the conversion of the first Gentile Christians (Acts 10). After a time when the gospel was for Jews only, Peter was sent by God to give the gospel to Cornelius and his household. They were gloriously converted and even spoke in tongues as proof.

When Peter returned to the community of Hebrew Christians, he discovered they were displeased with his having preached to Gentiles. They were distressed at the prospect of having to accept these pork-eaters as brothers. Peter filled them in on the whole story, saying, "And as I began to speak, the Holy Ghost fell on them, as on us at the beginning" (Acts 11:15). These last six words probably refer to the Pentecost tongues, because Acts 10:46 tells us that the Jewish brothers who went along with Peter witnessed the new Gentile converts speaking in tongues. Without this sign, perhaps Peter could not have convinced the Hebrew Christians that God had really chosen to reach out to the Gentiles with the gospel.

There are episodes in the New Testament which were strictly introductory in nature. God was ushering in the dispensation of grace, the focal point of his love's handiwork on man's behalf, and he did many things differently by way of introduction. We cannot build doctrine as such on many of these introductory phenomena.

For instance, John the Baptist was filled with the Holy Ghost from his mother's womb. In Luke 1:15, 41 we are told that his mother was filled with the Holy Ghost when Mary came into the room, and the baby John then leapt within her. As far as I know, no one has ever tried to build any doctrine on this experience. We recognize it as being introductory in nature.

In 1 Corinthians 12:28-30, the Apostle Paul lists spiritual gifts, starting with apostleship and ending with tongues. In this passage, Paul tells us clearly that we can't assume that all Christians filled with the Holy Ghost will speak in tongues — which was perhaps to some degree an introductory gift. "Are all apostles? Are all prophets? Are all teachers? Are all workers of miracles? Have all gifts of healing? Do all speak with tongues? Do all interpret?" Paul goes on in the next chapter to point out one unmistakable sign that we will have when we make our lives 100 percent available to God — and that is love.

When you accepted Christ and became a real Christian, you probably thanked him for what he did and invited him to come into your heart to live. In view of Romans 6, have you said a prayer thanking him that your "old man" was put to death on the Cross and that you were raised to be alive to God through Jesus Christ our Lord? Understanding and trusting this, have you asked him to come in and assume full control?

Driving a standard-transmission car illustrates this. You let out on the clutch and in on the accelerator as one simultaneous effort. The "old man" out and Christ in. Now what? Do I shift again?

No, turn to 1 Thessalonians 5:16-19. There are some things mentioned here that folks who are driving along 100 percent in the power of the Spirit should be doing. These aren't just a new set of rules, but things that will for the most part happen spontaneously. They can be considered reminders of what the abundant life is really all about.

Verse 16 says, "Rejoice evermore." This should be quite natural for someone who realizes that he doesn't have to sin any more, because the "old man" is dead and Christ is at the controls. There is nothing harder for someone outside the Spirit to do. Rejoice some of the time, once in a while, but not as a habit — that's the maxim of many.

Verse 17 says, "Pray without ceasing." This does not mean that you should go around mumbling pieties all day. It is an attitude of prayer, an attitude of dependence. It includes not worrying about a problem you have, because you have already turned it over to God and you are quite confident in his capability to handle it. Even more, you're confident that he wants to handle it.

We want to be quick to turn these things over to God, not stopping to worry over each one. You might say the abundant life relies on quick turnover. How fast can you say, "Lord, I have a problem"? That's how long you should keep it to yourself. As long as you go about your daily living in that frame of mind, you are in the attitude of praying without ceasing.

Verse 18 states, "In every thing give thanks: for this is the will of God in Christ Jesus concerning you." Man, that would really be tough without the Spirit. But he's with us, so praise the Lord for that flat tire. He had a reason for allowing it. You may get a chance to witness about Christ to the fellow who helps you change it, and you told God that you were available to do just that. I hope that you didn't place any limitations on your availability — like not on a lonely road, or at night, or in the rain. You may not be able always to see the reasons for everything, but there is another familiar verse which might help make it even more clear:

"And we know that all things work together for good to them that love God, to them who are the called according to his purpose" (Romans 8: 28). Don't overlook that little clause on the end — "who are the called according to his purpose."

Many Christians seem to miss that last point and go skipping through a self-centered life questioning the truthfulness of that verse. If your life is turned over to him as he intended from the beginning, then you are "the called according to his purpose." Consequently everything will work together for good in your life, because God said it would. This may not appear to be the case, but by faith you know it's true.

Then there should be no reason to balk at the admonition of 1 Thessalonians 5:18 — "in everything give thanks." A college girl once paraphrased this verse: "Thank you, Lord, for a rotten day." Of course, if we really make our lives available to God, things that could ruin our day don't have to, because we can punt our problems to God. In Christ we can have a good day every day.

Giving thanks for everything doesn't mean that we can go whizzing along through life on the wrong side of the road, trusting God to endorse our stupidity by causing everyone else to pull off onto the shoulder. But it does mean that we can give thanks for things that we used to look on as tribulations, because we are now in God's will and this is his way of using us. Thank you, Jesus!

The last of these four verses (19) in 1 Thessalonians 5 says, "Quench not the Spirit." How can you know when the Spirit is speaking? Aren't you walking in the Spirit? If you have turned everything over to the Lord, where do you think that still, small voice comes from?

Now I'm not talking about whatever it is that gives you such routine instructions as it's time to eat or it's time to go to bed. I'm speaking of the voice that says, "Did you know that Joe Jones is really searching for something in his life? We both know it's Christ. So be alert because I'm going to tell him about Christ through you." Or the voice that says, "Why don't you give Mary Smith a call? I want to tell her something with your lips." It's when we say, "Sorry, Holy Spirit, you'll have to find another mouth. I stutter," that we "quench the Spirit."

Galatians 5:16 gives the positive side of this

negative command: "This I say then, Walk in the Spirit, and ye shall not fulfil the lust of the flesh." In other words, we can get so carried away with representing the Lord that we become absolutely absent-minded toward the old things that used to take up our time.

Before long we can look back and be startled at not having even thought about doing some of the things that used to really turn us on. Of course, that's when we really begin to live — when these artificial things drop off. When we live for Christ and not just for a new car, boat, boyfriends, fishing, bowling, or you name it, then we are alive, really alive!

Are you still just a little worried about a sign to confirm the reality of your faith? Just do what God said to do — present your whole life; don't polish up the "old man." You have no reason to suppose that it "won't take." You have the Word of God to stand on. "You need to keep on patiently doing God's will if you want him to do for you all that he has promised" (Hebrews 10:36).

Be patient, trust God to make your life blossom. He'll change your life right before your eyes — and your neighbors' eyes as well. But watch out for pride. One sometimes wonders about people who feel compelled to stress how long they have been filled with the Holy Spirit!

One of the manifestations of the Holy Ghost is that he witnesses with our spirits (Romans 8:16). He witnesses to God about our justification and our sanctification, but he witnesses to us as well.

To put it in a twentieth-century word, he actualizes our experiences.

Look at Ephesians 3:16-19. These are strong and wonderful words that tell us again that we no longer need a sign, because we have the Holy Spirit in us actualizing or confirming our experience of faith.

> (16) That out of his glorious, unlimited resources he will give you the mighty inner strengthening of his Holy Spirit. (17) And I pray that Christ will be more and more at home in your hearts, living within you as you trust in him. May your roots go down deep into the soil of God's marvelous love, (18, 19) and may you be able to feel and understand, as all God's children should, how long, how wide, how deep, and how high his love really is; and to experience this love for yourselves, though it is so great that you will never see the end of it or fully know or understand it. And so at last you will be filled up with God himself.   (TLB)

The more we become available for filling with the Holy Ghost, the more he is able to say, "I told you so. I told you in my Word that if you would reckon the 'old man' dead, I would come in and take over." So all we need now is patience to let God keep his promises in us.

Chapter Seven

Will I Still Sin?

Yes, you will. But that isn't the end of the road. Sin is still treated exactly the same as before — confess it quickly. Maybe you're thinking, "Funny, if the 'old man' was crucified (Romans 6:6) and I followed the admonition of Romans 6:11 and reckoned it so, and if the 'old man' is what causes me to sin, well, why do I still sin?" Sounds like a lot of doubletalk.

The "old man" was crucified, "that the body of sin might be destroyed" (Romans 6:6). Remember, "destroyed." Verse 14 says, "For sin shall not have dominion over you." It can't — it was destroyed, utterly defeated, vanquished, made of no effect. Hence we are told, "Reckon ye also yourselves to be dead indeed unto sin" (Romans 6:11).

When someone dies, his body has no more life and has started that irreversible process of decomposition. The body was, but is no more. If the "old man" died in this way, he could not have been born in us at our physical birth. He was, though. If the "old man" became a corpse after our spiritual regeneration, he could have no effect upon us whether we reckoned him so or not. But he does have an effect on us.

Obviously we are to reckon the "old man" dead for a different reason. Satan, sin, death, and hell were all defeated at Calvary. We reckoned it so for salvation. We know how it will all turn out in the end. Satan will be cast into the lake of fire and we Christians will all live forever in heaven with God.

True; but Satan *was* defeated, and our "old man" *is* crucified. We have probably been viewing all this as though it *will* take place. We tend to place this in the future because the actual execution of these events is all tied in with prophecy that is yet to happen.

The important thing is this — Christ had victory over all the forces of evil at Calvary and their power over us was broken. It was broken if we reckon it so. Remember that Satan is a sore loser; he'll fight us every step of the way.

Am I saying that you can think Satan dead or the "old man" will be whatever you want him to be? No. If I were going to hand you that line, I'd have you start off with "Every day in every way I'm getting better and better!" Brainwashing is not what I'm advocating. I'm talking about facing facts.

If you were a bank manager and one of your tellers accepted a one-hundred-dollar check against the account of J. M. Smith, only to find out later that J. M. Smith had been dead for ten years, you would be put out with her, to say the least. If you didn't fire her, you would at least give her quite a lecture on negligence. Imagine anyone honoring a check signed by someone who has been dead for ten years!

Supposing you find yourself in the position that Paul describes in Romans 7:19 (Amplified): "For I fail to practice the good deeds I desire to do, but the evil deeds that I do not desire to do are what I am (ever) doing." This would be an admission that you reckon the "old man," who is supposedly dead, to have power over you, and because of this you are allowing him to live in your body and to have dominion over your life. There is only room for one person to have dominion, which, of course, leaves the Holy Spirit out. Not out of your life entirely, just out of control.

Are you accepting orders or checks signed "Old Man?" Check the records in Romans 6 — his account was closed out nearly two thousand years ago.

Let's look at one area that might give you a little more respect for Satan's forgery skills. "Pride" is a word that we sometimes give more than one meaning. We may feel that we have no right to feel pride in our looks or any other God-given asset. If we sing a good solo in the morning service, teach a good lesson in Sunday school, or preach a fine sermon, we try very hard to avoid basking in the compliments and instead say, "Praise the Lord." We have prayed for God to be glorified through us and he was, and we make every effort to make it perfectly clear that we want none of the glory.

We might, of course, in the privacy of our own thoughts say, "Yes, Holy Spirit, you sang a fine solo through me this morning and you deserve all the credit, but I don't think you could have been quite so effective through Mrs. So-and-so."

Of course, Satan tempts us to steal a little glory that we know we have no right to. Satan doesn't always have the success he would like here, because we have made up our minds and closed the door on that issue. It's just too cut and dried. So he tries another door.

Do you play a sport, work with your hands, or have a hobby? We are allowed to have pride in personal accomplishments. Or are we? It's easy to be proud of a seventy-six for eighteen holes — after all, that's only four over par. What about a seventy-pound sailfish, or an elk so large it's mentioned in the record books?

Pride is always relative. First we start off innocently enough by being proud of our one-pound fish, because it's the biggest thing we ever caught. We feel very humble by comparison when we see fish of that species as large as ten pounds. What happens to our hat size when we finally do catch a ten-pounder? Relatively speaking it's the largest one around which fosters pride. Pride is competitive.

What about pride in our nation, school, family, or church? Sounds innocent enough. It's not pride in one's self, anyway. Watch it. I'm proud of my wife and why shouldn't I be? I don't know of a better cook. She is a fantastic Bible teacher. She's charming and everyone loves her. People often tell me how much they appreciate her. Why do I enjoy hearing someone telling me what I already know about her? Because she's my wife and anything she does reflects well on me and makes me look just a little smarter than the average guy for being able to catch her. What do you think motivates a child to say, "My daddy can whip your daddy"? The same thing that would cause me to say my wife outclasses yours. Pride. Pride by association.

I'm not trying to demote you to sackcloth and ashes, only to give some food for thought. It's good to check our motives once in a while.

Not all the things mentioned here are necessarily sin, but if you think about it there surely is room for Satan to slip in a forgery to drag the old nature out for a breath of fresh air.

Romans 12:3 gives some fine advice on this subject: "For by the grace (unmerited favor of God) given to me I warn every one among you not to estimate and think of himself more highly than he ought — not to have an exaggerated opinion of his own importance; but to rate his ability with sober judgment, each according to the degree of faith apportioned by God to him" (Amplified).

Even more important, if you should find yourself getting a bit puffed up, confess it. Keep coming back to 1 John 1:9; confession of sin is essential for spiritual growth.

But don't sit in a corner, worrying about making a misstep. People who don't make mistakes usually don't do anything. Yes, we have just finished a long discussion on how slick Satan is, but don't forget that standard transmission. Remember when you let out on the clutch, you press in on the accelerator, unless you want to kill the motor. When you reckoned the "old man" dead, you also reckoned yourself alive unto Christ. You didn't just get rid of the "old man" and leave a void. You now have Christ, through the Holy Spirit, and he will be in complete control — as complete as you will allow. Satan may be able to fool you, but he can't fool Jesus.

I have developed an appreciation for the Holy Spirit. One of his jobs is to convict me of sin, and he does all of his work well. Sometimes I'm made aware that the Holy Spirit is shaking his finger at me and saying, "David, you have a sin to confess," and I say, "Yes, sir," and confess it. Then I am made aware that the same arm that was rebuking me is now around my shoulder as we walk on down the road. The Holy Spirit dwells in me, and he is not so remote that he can't put his arm around me and love me. That's another one of his jobs — he is the Comforter, so I would never want to quench him.

In fact, he has made me so comfortable in the Lord that I can rejoice evermore, pray without ceasing, and in all things give thanks, because I know that this is the will of God for me.